# Resource Stewardship Strategy Pilot Review

*Natural Resource Stewardship and Science Directorate*

Natural Resource Report NPS/NRSS/NRR—2011/412

Guy Adema

Denali National Park and Preserve
PO Box 9
Denali Park, AK 99755

David Vana-Miller and
Don Weeks

Natural Resource Stewardship and Science
PO Box 2527
Denver, CO 80225

June 2011

U.S. Department of the Interior
National Park Service
Natural Resource Stewardship and Science
Fort Collins, Colorado

The National Park Service, Natural Resource Stewardship and Science office in Fort Collins, Colorado publishes a range of reports that address natural resource topics of interest and applicability to a broad audience in the National Park Service and others in natural resource management, including scientists, conservation and environmental constituencies, and the public.

The Natural Resource Report Series is used to disseminate high-priority, current natural resource management information with managerial application. The series targets a general, diverse audience, and may contain NPS policy considerations or address sensitive issues of management applicability.

All manuscripts in the series receive the appropriate level of peer review to ensure that the information is scientifically credible, technically accurate, appropriately written for the intended audience, and designed and published in a professional manner.

This report received informal peer review by subject-matter experts who were not directly involved in the collection, analysis, or reporting of the information.

Views, statements, findings, conclusions, recommendations, and data in this report do not necessarily reflect views and policies of the National Park Service, U.S. Department of the Interior. Mention of trade names or commercial products does not constitute endorsement or recommendation for use by the U.S. Government.

This report is available from and the Natural Resource Publications Management website (http://www.nature.nps.gov/publications/nrpm/).

Please cite this publication as:

NPS 999/108032, June 2011

# Contents

# Appendices

# Executive Summary

This paper summarizes the 2010 evaluation of the process used to develop Natural Resource Stewardship Strategy (RSS) reports for six diverse "pilot" parks in the National Park System. The successes and challenges documented here may be used to guide other parks as they undertake this planning process.

The most current information and guidance on Resource Stewardship Strategies, along with existing reports, presentations, and related materials, can be found on the NPS intranet site: http://www1.nrintra.nps.gov/planning/

## Background

The Natural Resource Stewardship Strategy (RSS) planning concept was formally initiated in fiscal year (FY) 2006 to develop comprehensive strategies for improved resource conditions, to guide investment toward those science-based strategies, and to improve fiscal accountability in resource management in the National Park System. The RSS design was a natural progression from Resource Management Plans, which recognized the dependent relationships of interdisciplinary management activities on resource condition. A core tenet of Resource Stewardship Strategies is that they are built on a sound scientific foundation and directly relate resource goals to founding principles of a park unit and National Park Service (NPS) management policies. RSSs provide a crucial link between General Management Plans (GMPs) and specific management activities, providing a 10-20 year roadmap for meeting a park unit's desired condition. Resource stewardship strategies provide guidance for managers, but do not provide the decisions addressed at the broad level by a GMP or at the implementation level by a specific project or activity.

Prototype, or pilot Resource Stewardship Strategies have been completed, or substantially completed, for six park units as of spring 2010. The Natural Resource Stewardship and Science (NRSS) leadership recognized the potential value of a formal evaluation of the various products completed by parks, including: the challenges and successes of the resource planning process; the effectiveness of interdisciplinary integration; and the overall value of the completed products. RSSs play a key role in condition based management and it is important to reflect on experiences of the development and implementation of the pilot plans prior to embarking on a long-term program.

The review of the pilot parks planning processes occurred from January through April of 2010 and consisted of interviews with key participants in completion of RSSs, meetings with advisory groups and workgroups, and a formal workshop with diverse representation from parks, Washington Support Office (WASO), regions, and the Denver Service Center(DSC). Interviews focused on the experience of those staff directly involved in completion of pilot RSS products. The RSSs from six park units most complete at the time of the review received the most attention, the experiences of those parks earlier in the process were also included. The pilots came from units with a range of designated purposes and included a diverse set of park purposes, including natural and cultural focused sites both large and small. The pilot parks with reviewable RSS drafts in spring 2010 were:

| | |
|---|---|
| – Herbert Hoover National Historic Site | (complete) |
| – Denali National Park and Preserve | (complete) |
| – Guadalupe Mountains National Park | (complete) |
| – Monocacy National Battlefield | (final draft) |
| – Chattahoochee River National Recreation Area | (reviewable draft) |
| – Point Reyes National Seashore | (reviewable draft) |

## Process

The pilot resource stewardship strategies each developed under unique circumstances and different approaches for completion. In addition to understanding the efficacy of pilot products to park management, it was important to understand the various development methods, unit-specific goals, and project management approach for each product. Pilot park staff, their regional coordinators, and WASO subject matter experts were all involved in each pilot product and had unique insight to the efficacy of the development process and resulting products.

Through a series of conference calls and personal interviews a set of recurring themes evolved which needed to be addressed and considered in a larger context. In addition to developing a set of powerful strategic plans for six parks, the pilots had highlighted the most valuable and complex aspects of comprehensive, long-term, interdisciplinary resource planning.

Those themes and related questions became the focus for a formal workshop. The workshop not only provided specific feedback to those parks involved, but also provided a forum to build consensus on the strengths of the RSS which should be included in future efforts, developed insight to improvements for future efforts, and identified key features of an effective program to guide an effective resource planning program.

The workshop was held April 13-15, 2010 in Ft Collins, Colorado and included 14 representatives from NPS field units, 8 representatives from WASO, seven representatives from regional management, and two representatives from the Denver Service Center. The diverse group included cultural and natural resource specialists and managers, superintendents, national program managers, and professional planners. The meeting was organized by eight thematic questions:

1. What are the consensus observations from pilot reports?
2. How do parks achieve interdisciplinary integration in resource planning?
3. What is the ideal relationship of RSS's to other planning and evaluation steps?
4. How do other planning efforts best integrate and complement the RSS?
5. What is the goal of Expert Review?
6. What is the best way to complete an RSS for various park situations?
7. What is the role of WASO Specialists to assist park RSS's?
8. RSS Program management: What support and leadership is ideal?

Through the groups analysis of pilot experiences, a complementary set of common themes emerged about resource stewardship strategies which lead to recommendations for the next phase of the program.

## Themes

### *Utility of RSS to Guide Resource Investment*

Upon detailed review of the pilot RSS products by the diverse group of workshop attendees, the value of the strategic planning process was unquestioned. Despite the great variety with each individual RSS, and regardless of the specific layout or focus of each RSS, each served a clear purpose for connecting resource activities to park purpose and provided the park direction for future activities. The pilot RSSs met the goal of expanding beyond traditional, project-heavy resource management plans, and met the challenge of having interdisciplinary and science-based comprehensive strategies. All participating parks and regional representatives lauded the value of having completed the RSS process.

### *Interdisciplinary Integration*

The Resource Stewardship Strategy is the best tool yet to help parks view all resources collectively and with a common goal. All parks saw substantial value to an interdisciplinary approach, though some were more successful than others. Review team expressed great interest in continuing an interdisciplinary approach, many consider it crucial.

### *RSS Sequencing – relation to other planning activities*

There are various ways to complete an RSS successfully. Having well defined fundamental resource values is critical to development of a RSS. The relation and sequencing of the RSS to related efforts such as natural resource condition assessments, climate change scenario planning, and social science was less definitive, but important to proactively consider during the RSS process.

### *Facilitation*

Pilot parks had good experiences with three models of RSS project management: facilitated by the park, facilitated by Denver Service Center, and facilitated by Natural Resource Stewardship and Science (NRSS) staff. Mixed success was reported from those using a cooperator-led approach. The most important element of facilitation was a clear understanding of the purpose of RSS's, strong management support, and a common desire to work toward more strategic management of park resources.

### *Role of WASO and NRPC*

WASO and NRPC staff played a key role in some pilot RSSs by providing common guidance in some discipline areas and project oversight. The value of a more coordinated role was clear to all who worked with RSSs. Cultural Resources has a more challenging structure to provide RSS support. Denver Service Center played a key role in ensuring completion of quality RSSs for some parks.

### *Program Management*

Parks completing pilot RSSs saw a need for a well-organized program to support parks and regions through the RSS process, particularly due to the uniqueness of the resource stewardship strategy relative to other park plans. Parks experienced variable levels of support, most would have preferred more guidance and examples. It was commonly felt that there needed to be some

RSS expertise within each region and some level of regional responsibility. It was suggested that NRPC could act as subject matter experts and provide guidance to parks.

## Recommendations

1. The Resource Stewardship Strategy should become a core element of resource management in NPS units. RSSs provide the foundation for resource investment and accountability, providing comprehensive, interdisciplinary, and science-based strategies to guide park activities.

2. Parks should carefully consider the order of operations in completing resource evaluation and planning steps to best meet their situation. A current General Management Plan or a formal statement of fundamental and other resource values should be a pre-requisite to initiating a Resource Stewardship Strategy. The order of completion of a natural resource condition assessment should be carefully considered and closely linked to the completion of a RSS.

3. The Resource Stewardship Strategy effort should transition from a project to a program. The program should have a dedicated lead at the WASO level and trained staff at the regional level to support RSS project management and facilitation.

4. The RSS program should be integrated with other resource evaluation efforts. A Director's Order and Reference Manual should be developed to put RSSs in context with all elements of the condition-based management initiative. The RSS should be a core element of a portfolio approach to planning which includes documents such as foundation statements, condition assessments, and periodic reporting elements.

5. National project funding sources should be made available for resource stewardship strategy funding, recognizing that each RSS process will have different costs depending on park size, complexity, and project approach. The national program manager should develop collaborative efforts as appropriate to assist parks in accessing appropriate fund sources.

6. Standardize the product suite for Resource Stewardship Strategies. Parks should be required to (1) produce a concise, pre-defined report to meet WASO management needs, and (2) produce a comprehensive document with prescribed main sections and key elements, and be encouraged to (3) produce a park-specific product aimed at sharing their RSS with partners, stakeholders, visitors, and/or staff. The requirements of items (1) and (3) should be well documented with adequate examples and functional templates.

7. A standardized database tool should be developed for creation of activity sequencing and budget estimation.

8. Parks should be encouraged to keep their RSS current through periodic updates and progress reports. A concise and simple template should be made available.

9. Develop clear guidance for expert review and a cohort of consistent reviewers to ensure RSS products meet the service-wide intent while still being locally relevant and scientifically robust.

10. Maintain current momentum and enthusiasm of parks that have recently completed or are near completion of an RSS. Encourage mentorship of other parks in their regions. Develop a long-term comprehensive program funding strategy, but also find a way to maintain a core program with steadily improving products.

11. Solidify interdisciplinary support of RSS approach to resource planning. Continue product development to integrate existing evaluation and reporting processes from cultural resources, maintenance interpretation, education, and law enforcement to maximize the value and effectiveness of the identified comprehensive strategies.

12. Allow parks creativity within the framework of the RSS to develop new ways approaching management of emerging issues, such as climate change scenario planning, wilderness management, changing social conditions, and other complex issues which transcend all aspects of park management.

13. WASO disciplines should provide subject matter expertise to all parks. Discipline-specific planning guidance should be provided in a standard format through a convenient portal. Guidance for standard indicators, potential reference conditions, and possible strategies should address both data-rich and data-poor parks. Parks should be provided a facilitator at the WASO level to help interpret guidance, but also to help parks find additional guidance when appropriate.

# Introduction

The Natural Resource Stewardship Strategy (RSS) planning concept has been in a development phase since production of a draft Director's Order 2.1 (DO-2.1): *Resource Stewardship Planning* in 2005. Prototype Resource Stewardship Strategies have been completed, or substantially completed, for a number of parks and NRSS leadership recognized the value in a formal evaluation of the various products completed by parks, including the challenges and success of the resource planning process, effectiveness of interdisciplinary integration, and overall value of the completed products.

The review occurred from January through April of 2010 and consisted of interviews with key participants in completion of RSSs, meetings with advisory groups and workgroups, and a formal workshop with diverse representation from parks, WASO, regions, and the Denver Service Center.

The review process focused on six Resource Stewardship Strategies. Interviews and the workshop used these examples to provide insight to strengths and weaknesses not only of the individual RSSs, but of the overall approach to completion of an RSS, contents of an RSS, project management of an RSS, and leadership of a servicewide RSS program.

## RSS Objectives

The objectives of a RSS are well established in draft Director's Order DO-2.1, Resource Stewardship Planning. Among other things, draft DO-2.1 establishes the purpose, authority, required components, environmental planning considerations, and definitions for RSSs. While only a draft document, substantial guidance for the implementation of a comprehensive resource planning program is presented.

The objectives were further interpreted in a briefing sheet revised most recently in October 2007, Appendix 2 (Mason, 2007). Mason (2007) presents the core tenets of this revised approach to resource planning, including a vision for improved accountability, a replacement for traditional Resource Management Plan (RMP), and the integrative nature envisioned for the RSS:

> "Consistent with the current NPS Park Planning Framework is a category of park-specific "park program plans" that tier directly off of the park General Management Plan (GMP). Included among these plans is the park's Resource Stewardship Strategy (RSS), a document designed to provide (1) an objective basis for assessing the condition of natural and cultural resources relative to the "desired conditions" established in the park GMP, and (2) to document science- and scholarship-based comprehensive strategies to achieve and maintain these desired conditions. These subject-matter expert reviewed strategies consist of a logical sequence over time of general and interrelated activities determined to be necessary to advance, if not actually achieve or maintain, the current condition of a park's resources toward their desired conditions."

The objectives of the RSS had been well articulated, but it was widely recognized that implementation of the plans would be complicated across the diverse types of parks in the NPS.

## RSS Background and Status

It was understood that implementation of DO-2.1 would be complex and pilot efforts were needed to establish a suitable set of guidance prior to acceptance of service-wide policy. A Fee Demonstration (20%) project was established to complete improved RSS guidance and a set of pilot RSS products. The first pilot RSS funded through this project was Herbert Hoover National Historic Site (HEHO), completed in 2006. In cooperation with NRSS staff, HEHO also produced a template and handbook as a guide to help ensuing parks. The HEHO example, template, and handbook provided substantial insight to the principles articulated in DO-2.1, but left many questions unanswered.

It was recognized that HEHO was a single site in a diverse system of NPS units with highly variable resource attributes, degrees of staff specialization, knowledge of resources, and public interest. Compounding the natural diversity of parks is the disparity in the stage of management planning in each of the units.

Eight parks were selected for funding pilot RSSs between FY 2006 and FY 2008. Those parks were:

- Herbert Hoover National Historic Site (HEHO)
- Denali National Park and Preserve (DENA)
- Guadalupe Mountains National Park (GUMO)
- Effigy Mounds National Monument (EFMO)
- Monocacy National Battlefield (MONO)
- Chattahoochee River National Recreation Area (CHAT)
- New River Gorge National River (NERI)
- Point Reyes National Seashore (PORE)

Six of the eight parks had either completed or showed significant process on their RSSs at the end of FY 2009. Those six expressed a perception of great value in their product, but all had encountered different challenges in completing their projects, and each had developed particular elements unique to their RSS.

The pilots also used a variety of approaches to project management for completion of their RSS, including expanding on existing park resources (DENA, MONO, PORE, HEHO), using a dedicated facilitator from Denver Service Center (GUMO, CHAT), and using non-NPS contractors (NERI). The EFMO RSS process was terminated prior to completion so the park could focus on other planning efforts. Each approach had unique implications for impacts on park staff and cost. Because the pilot RSSs used a cross-section of available methods, it was possible to gain reasonable insight to the pros and cons of each method.

As of the writing of this report, sixteen park units had initiated an RSS process, of which three had been completed. A full status report is included in Appendix 1 and summarized in the table below.

While the first eight RSSs were funded from NRSS-directed funds (with the exception of DENA, which used substantial supplementary park funding), subsequent RSSs were not. Those had to develop park-specific project statements for completion in various fund sources, or fund their effort from existing park base funds.

**Summary Status of RSS Efforts (as of June 2011)**

| Unit | Region | Start FY | Finish FY | Method | Status |
|---|---|---|---|---|---|
| Herbert Hoover NHS | MWR | 2006 | 2007 | Self | Complete |
| Denali NP & P | AKR | 2006 | 2009 | Self | Complete |
| Guadalupe Mountains NP | IMR | 2007 | 2009 | DSC | Complete |
| Effigy Mounds NM | MWR | | | Self | Process terminated |
| Monocacy NB | NCR | 2006 | 2010 | Self | Complete |
| Chattahoochee River NRA | SER | 2007 | 2011 | DSC | Review Draft |
| New River Gorge NR | NER | | 2011 | Contract | In Process |
| Point Reyes NS | PWR | 2006 | 2010 | Self | Review Draft |
| Klondike Gold Rush NHP | AKR | 2009 | 2011 | DSC | Review Draft |
| Sand Creek Massacre NHS | IMR | 2009 | 2011 | DSC | Review Draft |
| Lava Beds NM | PWR | 2010 | 2011 | Self | Review Draft |
| Abraham Lincoln Birthplace NHS | SER | 2010 | 2010 | DSC | Kickoff Mar10 |
| Valley Forge NHP | NER | 2008 | 2012 | NRPC | In process |
| Pecos NHP | IMR | 2010 | 2011 | CESU | Complete |
| Bering Land Bridge NP | AKR | 2010 | | | Insufficient funds for FY10 start |
| Pea Ridge NMP | MWR | 2010 | | | Insufficient funds for FY10 start |
| Catoctin Mountain Park | NCR | 2010 | | | Insufficient funds for FY10 start |
| Channel Islands NP | PWR | | | | Insufficient funds for FY10 start |
| Fort Donelson NB | SER | 2010 | | | Self-funded, starting in FY10 |
| Fort Union | MWR | Unknown | | | |
| Minuteman NM | NER | Unknown | | | |
| Boston Harbor Islands NRA | NER | | | | In process |
| Curecanti NRA | IMR | | | CESU | |

3

## Prior RSS Analyses

Prior to this RSS pilot and programmatic review, two efforts were made to share the lessons learned of pilot RSS efforts.

Malone and Cahill (2008) produced *Lessons Learned from the Pilot Resource Stewardship Strategy (RSS) Projects for Improving the Park Planning Program*, a report from the Denver Service Center (DSC) Planning Division to the WASO Office of Park Planning & Special Studies (PSS) and other relevant program offices. The study consisted of ten phone interviews conducted by the authors with RSS contacts using a standard set of questions. The qualitative findings from the interviews were presented in four areas:

(1) Value of the RSS;
(2) GMP Elements: Fundamental and Other Important Resources and Values;
(3) GMP Elements: Management Zones and Desired Conditions; and
(4) Needed Improvements to Guidance for GMPs and RSSs.

Malone and Cahill (2008) provided valuable feedback to NPS management involved in the evolution of the RSS concept, including many specific items for possible improvement. Many of the ideas presented in Malone and Cahill (2008) were echoed during this review effort.

Denn (2009) presented the results of an informal questionnaire of RSS issues completed by RSS pilot parks. The survey was intended to facilitate idea sharing and insight to how RSS parks were implementing various elements of the existing RSS guidance. Pilot parks responded to a range of 27 questions and provided their perspectives. While no attempt was made to find consensus among respondents or generate formal program recommendations, the survey served its purpose by fostering sharing of perspectives on RSS topics for others to gain insight to the process. Like Malone and Cahill (2008), many of the topics mentioned in Denn (2009) were also evident in this review.

In both Malone and Cahill (2008) and Denn (2009), parks reported that the overall process was worthwhile and helps tie resource work to a parks fundamental purpose. Both also highlighted the importance of having adequate foundation documents in place to have a successful RSS effort. That was clearly repeated during this review. Malone and Cahill (2008) also reported that parks found that organizing target conditions and strategies by management zone as established in a park's GMP was not highly useful and generally abandoned the effort.

Malone and Cahill (2008) summarized a number of "needed improvements to guidance for GMPs and RSSs". Suggestions included clarifying the audience for the RSS handbook, more formally including adaptive management as an element of the RSS framework, focusing the summary of current knowledge section on fundamental resources, modifying or eliminating the recommended use of management zones, and documenting indicators and target values. Similar to results from this review, they also suggested prioritization of comprehensive strategies, developing a better tool for cost estimation and timing, and clarifying the review process. The recommendations that Malone and Cahill (2008) developed are consistent with those developed during this review. In many cases, as more parks developed RSS experience, those areas in need of improvement became even clearer.

# Review of Pilot Resource Stewardship Strategies

## Interviews

In order to gather a consensus on the areas of deliberation for the pilot RSSs and RSS program, a series of interviews were conducted during January and February with park, regional, and WASO staff. Meetings occurred with representatives from each program area in Natural Resource Stewardship and Science Directorate, the natural and cultural Resource Stewardship Coordinators from each region, Denver Service Center Staff who had facilitated or were actively facilitating completion of Resource Stewardship Strategies, and park staff who had direct experience with RSSs. Questions and discussion were wide-ranging, but a consistent set of themes emerged which showed significant commitment to the fundamental concept of establishing a strategic planning process that linked park activities to park purposes.

A common set of questions emerged from the interviews which would form the framework of the pilot review:

1. What are the consensus observations from pilot reports?
2. How do parks achieve interdisciplinary integration in resource planning?
3. What is the ideal relationship of RSSs to other planning and evaluation steps?
4. How do other planning efforts best integrate and complement the RSS?
5. What is the goal of expert review?
6. What is the best way to complete an RSS for various park situations?
7. What is the role of WASO Specialists to assist park RSSs?
8. RSS Program management: What support and leadership is ideal?

## Workshop

A workshop was convened in Ft Collins, Colorado in April 2010 to focus the experience of those staff with direct experience either developing, advising, or working with RSSs on the thematic questions which evolved during the interviews. A large amount of the staff who played leadership roles in RSS efforts were either present or represented at the workshop, with a full agenda and attendance list in Appendices 3 and 4, respectively. Attendees included NRSS staff, NRPC program managers and division chiefs, regional RSS coordinators, staff who developed pilot RSSs, Denver Service Center RSS facilitators, and regional advisors. A mix of cultural and natural resource parks and attendees provided diverse insight on integration challenges, along with a mix of larger and smaller parks, and parks with larger and smaller staffs were represented.

The workshop began with a review of each available RSS product. Pilot parks presented the unique elements, strengths, and specific utility of their RSS. The group then discussed each RSS and provided feedback on which elements appeared to be most successful.

Parks with pilot Resource Stewardship Strategies were asked to present the highlights of their strategy to the workshop participants with special emphasis on the following items:

1) Your park's process - why you did an RSS, process for completion (staff, time, use of subject matter experts (SMEs), cost.), review, etc.
2) Overview of your park's RSS - structure, unique elements, most challenging part, etc.

3) Most useful elements of your RSS to park management.
4) Lease useful elements of your RSS and/or least efficient to complete.
5) Highlight - an element of your RSS which you find particularly innovative, practical, or interesting.
6) Specific areas in which you found the guidance and resulting RSS elements very useful and instructive.
7) Specific areas in which the guidance was not helpful to your process or did not provide adequate instruction.
8) What would you have improved or added if you had more time.
9) What's next - how has your park used the RSS to date, further plans for implementation, plans to keep RSS current.
10) Reflections - was it worth it?

Workshop participants were then asked to evaluate pilot RSSs with observations in four areas based on individual observations and evaluation by breakout groups:

1) Pilot RSS Elements: What are the most and least useful elements of each pilot product?
2) Innovations: Are there of innovative ideas from a pilot worth adopting programmatically?
3) Guidance: What are the reported and observed strengths and weakness of guidance?
4) Specifics: What specific change in guidance would have produced a better product?

Feedback on the individual RSS products varied substantially in the specific format and content by park. Different groups evaluated each pilot product and depending on their level of familiarity, were able to focus on specific issues unique to a pilot RSS rather than on the overall document. The overall result was successful, as all reviewers were well versed in the details of at least one pilot RSS and had engaged in deliberation around a particular aspect of at least one of the products. The collective outcome was that the group was able to develop a comparative analysis of the pilot products, evaluate their general efficacy for various parks, and most importantly, develop a sound foundation from which to make overall program recommendations.

Following presentation of individual RSSs, the group had developed a strong vernacular to discuss the core themes of the RSS review, including overall utility of an RSS, interdisciplinary integration, program management, climate change treatment, expert review, and overall programmatic needs. Those discussions resulted in many of the recommendations presented in this report.

## Themes

### *Utility of RSS to Guide Resource Investment*
The value of the strategic planning process was unquestioned by workshop attendees. Despite the great variety with each individual RSS, and regardless of the specific layout or focus of each RSS, each served a clear purpose for connecting resource activities to park purpose and provided the park direction for future activities. The pilot RSSs met the goal of expanding beyond traditional, project-heavy resource management plans, and met the challenge of having

interdisciplinary and science-based comprehensive strategies. All participating parks and regional representatives lauded the value of having completed the RSS process.

A clear consensus emerged of all interviewees and workshop participants that a clear framework for resource planning was critical for effective integrated resource management. There were concerns that the scope of RSSs was large enough that it precluded a quick and easy solution for parks and suggested various levels of interest for a shortened product which would guide a park prior to completion of an RSS. While a shortened strategy may suite short-term needs for project planning, the RSS process and format ensure that plans are scientifically sound and interdisciplinary in nature. Enough value was recognized in each of the pilot RSSs to recommend that parks embark on a RSS as soon as park staff and resources are available.

### Interdisciplinary Integration
The Resource Stewardship Strategy is the best tool yet to help parks view all resources collectively and with a common goal. All parks saw substantial value to an interdisciplinary approach, though some were more successful than others. Workshop attendees expressed great interest in continuing an interdisciplinary approach, and many consider it crucial.

Interviews with park and regional staff prior to the workshop had targeted sections to assess the value of interdisciplinary integration and a special section of the workshop explored the value and challenges of interdisciplinary integration. The largest area of integration was with natural and cultural resources, but considerations for other fields such as maintenance, law enforcement, and education were also discussed.

Presentations by Kathy Billings (PECO), Cheryl Sams-O'Neill (NER), Joy Beasly (MONO), Fred Armstrong (GUMO), Jeanne Schaff (AKR), and Philip Hooge (DENA) all highlighted outstanding successes in integration, each showing examples where an interdisciplinary approach is critical for successful resource management. Some pilot RSSs were more successful than others at full integration, but there was considerable interest in continuing on a collective approach.

Having interdisciplinary comprehensive strategies was noted to be of particular importance. The comprehensive strategies clearly show the involvement of many park activities in meeting resource goals, regardless of management division or funding source. It not only allowed resource staff to recognize how many activities affected resource condition, but also allowed for creative input by non-resource staff on resource management and protection. RSSs allow nearly all park staff to see where their work directly or indirectly leads to attainment of park goals.

### RSS Sequencing – relation to other planning activities
There are various ways to complete an RSS successfully. Having well defined fundamental resource values is critical to development of a RSS. The relation and sequencing of the RSS to related efforts such as natural resource condition assessments, climate change scenario planning, and social science was less definitive, but important to proactively consider during the RSS process.

All who participated in a RSS process reported that they felt it was critical that a park have either a current GMP, a current Foundation Statement, or at a minimum, a park-approved list of

Fundamental Resource Values and Other Important Resource Values in place. After that prerequisite, there were reasons presented why having a document and process like a Natural Resource Condition Assessment (NRCA) completed prior to starting a RSS is beneficial and other reasons why some thought that a NRCA should come before a RSS.

Overall consensus for best practice is to have a NRCA precede an RSS in order to help a park arrange their concept of resource condition around a set of indicators, providing a common language and foundation of thought to begin an RSS. KLGO is an example of a park which took this approach (and actually put their RSS on hold to complete their NRCA) and reported that it was a very positive experience.

### Facilitation

It is clear from the pilot examples that successful completion of a RSS requires a dedicated project manager and facilitator. Pilot parks had good experiences with three models of RSS project management: facilitated by the park, facilitated by Denver Service Center, and facilitated by NRPC staff. Mixed success was reported from partnership with university entities acting as the primary project manager. The NPS resource stewardship framework, including the RSS, has a complex enough framework that future RSS efforts should work to develop a network of project managers and facilitators with specialized skillsets.

In order to develop a readily-available cadre of experienced project manager/facilitators with the RSS-specific experience and sensitivities to the various NPS regions and their priorities, we recommend that in addition to Denver Service Center continuing their leadership of project management and facilitation, that each region's RSS coordinator also be a project manager and facilitator. Different regions will have different levels of capacity to make this possible without further funding, but with further RSS funding, establishing RSS coordinators who can also lead projects will allow for the RSS learning process and product evolution to continue while also building a team within the NPS who would become the core of resource strategic planning.

### Products

A standard suite of products is needed from RSS efforts. The workshop resulted in recommendations for two required RSS products and a third optional product. The products suite is designed to support the scientific integrity of the RSS process while also providing a readily communicated tool – necessary for non-resource staff, regional and WASO program managers, and non-NPS groups.

The first required product would be a short (2-5 pages) summary which includes a synopsis of a park's fundamental resources and values, the primary resource indicators, status, and targets, overall strategies for achievement, and basic timeline and budget information. The report format would be strictly guided by a template, not only making completion rather easy for the parks, but also allow for quick comparison and summary across regions or other groups as desired.

The second required report would be the actual Resource Stewardship Strategy, primarily in the same format which the pilots have already completed. A template would provide overall chapter structure and general direction, but parks would have the ability to develop the details of their RSS as needed. Adequate space for creativity should be allowed (and encouraged), but care should also be taken to ensure that parks were using scientific principles and fundamental values as the key component of RSS development.

The third potential RSS product would be an optional interpretive document. The first example of this type of document was presented by DENA. The purpose of this optional document would be to communicate the RSS to a broader group of interested people or groups than would be interested in the complete RSS, but would want more insight to the targets and strategies than provided in the short RSS brief. Local advocacy and education groups, non-resource park and regional staff, and scientifically-inclined visitors could be the expected audiences. A park could also target this report toward any one highly-influential or engaged partner, perhaps as an opportunity to highlight a partnership or roadmap for treatment of a particular resource management issue.

### Expert Review

Expert review is a key component of the RSS, ensuring that a professional peer group supports that the overall set of comprehensive strategies is a scientifically-sound approach to reach desired resource targets. Pilot parks reported a common set of challenges with the expert review process and developed a consensus idea that a network of expert reviewers will need to be established to accommodate timely, consistent, and meaningful review of RSSs. This professional cohort would be directed to focus on overall strategies and provide feedback to a park on the scientific integrity and completeness of their RSS.

This level of expert review is recommended to avoid revisiting more detailed sections of the indicators and targets which can be proactively sent for a review to discipline experts during the RSS process. In some cases, indicators and targets may already be peer-reviewed through an Inventory and Monitoring (I&M) or NRCA process. Parks should have discretion to send selected discipline-specific sections of their RSS for topic review at whichever phase is most helpful, essentially enlisting reviewers to become part of their subject matter expert input network.

By establishing a cadre of peer reviewers, it is less likely that reviewers will become bogged down with understanding the progression of laws, regulations, and policies affecting a park. Consistent reviewers will also develop an understanding of typical indicators and related NPS guidance, increasing efficiency and timeliness of reviews.

It's important that expert reviewers be selected which do not have a vested interest in the outcome of their review, such as university partners or common scientific cooperators. This aspect of the RSS process is important to retain the scientific integrity of the RSS, making it distinct from other typical NPS planning documents. With this, the RSS will be the central document in implementation of science-based management.

### Prioritization

While NRSS guidance for pilot RSSs discouraged ranking or banding of strategies, most pilot efforts found it internally useful for completion of their RSS. In fact, some pilot parks found the exercise one of the most important elements within the RSS process. Considerable caution was raised by NRSS leadership about prioritization of comprehensive strategies having potential to move the RSS closer to a decision document and away from a science document – that a RSS should simply provide the best scientifically recommended action to move an indicator toward a target value and not decide which management should pursue.

Pilot parks found that some sort of internal prioritization effort, whether ranking, banding, or otherwise categorizing strategies allowed them to realize the full value of their RSS effort. Parks reported their constant struggle with other interests to demonstrate the foundation for their work priorities. They found that an RSS provided that foundation without the fear of decision making or excess stipulation of a parks resulting actions, but provided the forum to develop a common understanding of the most important activities for resource management to impact resource condition.

No single example of a prioritization effort was shown to be superior to another. One unique approach included 'hedging', developed by PORE. Their hedging technique highlighted activities which would have a beneficial influence on a resource regardless if climate change impacts were as significant as expected or not. Therefore, they had a set of activities to move ahead with which would help the park resources whether the effects climate change proves to be a significant detriment or not.

The level and intensity of prioritization discussed to occur within a RSS is not close to that used for development of a 5-year plan or response to funding requests such as the Servicewide Comprehensive Call, but uses the knowledge gained from the RSS process to highlight those activities which are most likely to have a positive influence on the park's fundamental resources and values.

### *Support Tools: Timeline and Budget*
Pilot parks invested considerable time developing the timeline and budget sections of their pilot RSSs. The HEHO template provided an adequate framework, but parks found it inefficient to follow exactly, and when comparing pilots, it was clear that the pilots had considerably different interpretations of how detailed of an approach was appropriate for the budget and timeline sections.

The project timeline was helpful for parks to show that their strategies were realistically scheduled over the 10-20 period of relevancy of a RSS. The budget also showed that strategies were realistically designed and based on realistic funding scenarios. Taken together, this section can be a powerful tool to communicate the resource return on potential investment.

Given the considerable potential of this section of the RSS for communication to regions and WASO levels, it is recommended that a tool be developed for parks which allows for sequencing and budget estimation. The tool does not need to be complex, but help parks use common levels of estimation and detail, and allow parks and regions a comparable set of data for communication and provides parks the ability to easily update the core tables within the RSS as resource conditions, budgets, and costs change. It was clear that parks with smaller staffs had less ability to invest considerable time to formatting and tweaking the HEHO template to fit their specific situation, and reported that they would have greatly benefitted by having a database template.

Guidance accompanying any sequencing and budgeting tool should be definitive enough that data output from the tool in standard reports would be generally comparable across parks.

Common footnotes would also present the limits of extrapolation the schedule and budget beyond general long-term planning. The goal is not to develop another complex database which requires specialized knowledge and a steep learning curve, but a simple tool allowing visual development of Gantt charts for activities, their associated costs, and basic summary reports. A tool based in Microsoft Project or Access is envisioned, but could also be based on countless other platforms.

No need was identified for budget estimation beyond a class C level. The purpose of the budget exercise should remain a check on the reality of implanting the comprehensive strategies and showing the outstanding need for effective science-based management. Parks should be encouraged to evaluate all expected costs at a level which provides overall communication of the level of effort, but not at a level more typically prepared for Project Management Information System (PMIS) project statements or business plans.

### Living Document
Parks completing pilot RSSs almost universally wanted to see their efforts become part of a living document. Rather than completing a RSS and revisiting it in 10-20 years, after complete staff turnover and years of project work, they wanted to see the RSS take a form which could be regularly updated based on new information, new policy, or new efforts. Keeping an expert reviewed document under constant revision may be challenging, but if the updates are kept to timetable, budget, and reports in status of indicators, additional expert review may not be needed. Perhaps more realistic would be an annual or bi-annual (every two years) accomplishment report and update to the RSS, of a scope determined by park or regional management. The report could be as simple as showing which activities were on schedule and which were delayed, or complex and involve revisiting or indicators and standards. A reasonable expert review level would need to accompany revisions, but could be efficient if the same reviewers are available and changes are highlighted.

The obvious challenge to RSS reporting and revision is the staff time and energy required. Without the potential for project funding, the same cadre of project managers, DSC staff, or other key personnel may not be available for involvement. A simple annual reporting template could be created to facilitate regular reporting by resource managers on the status of their strategies and what changes are expected. This step should be closely coordinated with any pending changes to status of the parks reports, NRCA ongoing reporting, and other reporting efforts such as the cultural and archaeological reporting databases. Steps should be made so that any new reporting model either incorporate, or subsume existing reporting models. Every effort should be made to simplify park resource condition reporting to a level at which it will be completed regularly and accurately, but not so simple that it doesn't detect change in management strategies or resource condition.

### Climate Change, Wilderness, and Social Science
The pilot RSS products had different approaches to how they treated climate change, wilderness, and social science. Some embedded the topics within their approach to development of indicators and accompanying strategies while others explicitly discussed applicable aspects.

The consensus of the RSS workshop was that, in most foreseeable cases, climate change should be specifically addressed in an RSS. Because only a small number of RSSs have been completed and the NPS climate change response program is rapidly evolving, it was evident that flexibility is important at this stage of an RSS program. Each of the pilot RSSs treated climate change somewhat differently, but management mitigation and response measures were evident in every pilot RSS's comprehensive strategies.

Scenario planning is clearly a valuable tool to resource stewardship planning. Because the scenario planning program is nascent, it is not practical to define how it should fit in a RSS effort. What is clear is that there would be considerable value to having the results of a scenario planning exercise in hand when developing an RSS. A scenario planning exercise would also be valuable as a test of a set of defined comprehensive strategies.

Wilderness was only briefly addressed in this review effort due to other wilderness stewardship planning efforts and the overlap of wilderness stewardship with general management planning. While the approach of developing target conditions and strategies for those target conditions may be applicable to wilderness management goals, those strategies may have considerable overlap with other park planning efforts. Some elements of wilderness stewardship are likely appropriate to address in a RSS, but the review group recognized the necessary caution to avoid strategies which may directly, or indirectly, limit the decision frame for park uses.

### WASO Technical Support

WASO and regional discipline specialists have provided fundamental technical support in the completion of most pilot RSSs. Each pilot has received their support through slightly different channels and at different levels.

Parks reported a preference for each of the NRPC branches and relevant cultural resource specialties provided planning guidance in similar formats. Guidance could include exemplary sets of discipline-specific indicators and standards for both data-rich and data-poor parks. Example activities for improving condition would also be included. While parks would not be expected to adopt the example information directly, it would give parks ideas, language, and a sense of the range of information they should consider. Having examples in similar formats would make RSS preparation more efficient, and would make technical support effective.

In addition to providing guidance in a common format, parks found considerable value in having a NRPC staff person on their RSS team to help broker expertise within NRPC. The NRPC staff person would not have to be from a particular discipline - their main role would be to help ensure a consistent approach and to identify where additional input is available when needed.

Cultural resource management does not have a structure similar to NRPC. It would be helpful to parks if an inter-regional cultural resource team put together example guidance for how to best integrate existing cultural resource database information. Parks should not consider the RSS as a place to regurgitate existing cultural resource database information, but a place to evaluate all resources in an interdisciplinary context. In many ways, cultural resource elements have a stronger starting point by having existing databases from which to begin.

### Program Management

Parks completing pilot RSSs saw a need for a well-organized program to support parks and regions through the RSS process, particularly due to the uniqueness of the Resource Stewardship

Strategy relative to other park plans. While parks experienced variable levels of support, most would have preferred more guidance and examples. It was commonly felt that there needed to be some RSS expertise within each region and some level of regional responsibility. It was suggested that NRPC could act as subject matter experts and provide guidance to parks.

A national program lead is a clear necessity for successful implementation of an RSS program which will have longevity, consistency, and appropriate integration with other NPS programs. The national program manager location in a management structure is somewhat irrelevant as they would be expected to perform an interdisciplinary effort. The goals of the program manager would be to develop program guidance, provide leadership to parks and regions, advocate for program funding and collaboration with other servicewide efforts, and communicate the value of science-based interdisciplinary approach to resource management planning.

Parks and regions indicated a strong preference and perceived value of establishing RSS expertise within each region. A designated regional RSS lead would ideally be a project manager and facilitator, as well as provide oversight and advice to parks doing their own RSS or using Denver Service Center or other cooperators. By having the expertise within a region, sharing of subject matter expertise, regional expertise, and integration of regional goals would be more effectively facilitated than WASO-based planners. Proper implementation of a full RSS program would have a dedicated resource planner in each region.

### *Other Observations*
1. The RSS program needs strong regional and WASO leadership to become accepted, whether or not project funding is available.
2. Resource Stewardship Strategies should be considered as part of a holistic set of resource management tools. Their design and implementation should be thoughtfully organized within a portfolio planning and evaluation efforts including foundation statements, condition assessments, and related periodic reporting.
3. A Director's Order should encompass all planning efforts rather than just Resource Stewardship Strategies.
4. As new examples become available their strongest elements should be highlighted and shared widely.
5. A strong communication effort highlighting where parks have successfully implemented RSSs in management should be ongoing.
6. The RSS program should develop two strategies – one for a shorter-term implementation with current programmatic funding, and a complementary strategy developed to take full advantage of the potential RSSs with full funding. There is no need for parks to wait for programmatic funding to develop RSSs, but parks will need to find project funding if there is not capacity with existing park, regional, and/or WASO staff.
7. Environmental histories have been shown to provide very useful background for RSS development and can help with ensuring an interdisciplinary approach.
8. Wildland fire management goals need to play a strong role in development of an RSS and should not be overlooked.
9. Definitions of resource planning and evaluation terms should be maintained and communicated.
10. Examples of particularly effective RSS sections should be highlighted for various types of parks to help speed the learning curve for new RSS starts.

## Specific RSS Observations

Parks presented their experience developing an RSS along with observations to the review group. The group then discussed each of the RSSs and identified characteristics particularly evident or unique to that RSS. The collection of park's self-observations and the comments of the review group are listed below. These observations were, in total, the basic information which informed discussion themes and eventual recommendations.

### Herbert Hoover National Historic Site

*Chapters/ Main Elements: What are the most and least useful elements of the RSS?*

- Did a good job identifying information needs.
- Park reported that they used the comprehensive strategies.
- Informs when and how to develop project statements.
- Comprehensive strategies allowed the park to see what was next and allowed for preparation.
- RSS recognized different "languages "spoken by natural and cultural resource staff.
- Park found RSS helpful for developing PMIS statements.
- Helpful in relating program reports (e.g. CLR) to GMP, natural resource to bigger picture.
- Least useful element for the park was the budget exercise.

*Innovations: Are there of innovative ideas from the RSS worth adopting programmatically?*

Since HEHO was the first RSS, they felt that they would have benefitted greatly by having an example from which to work. State Historic Preservation Office SHPO involvement, budget refinement to encourage "living within your means", determining relationships between cultural and natural resource program elements were all innovations from the HEHO RSS. HEHO reported that having as many resource assessments as complete as possible would help the RSS process (i.e.: CLI, LCS, ASMIS, FMSS, vital signs).

*Guidance: What are the reported and observed strengths and weakness of guidance?*

HEHO reported that NEPA planners had trouble with compliance aspect of strategy. They were careful to include multiple cultural resource people, and worked to determine how to apply vital signs. Timeline, annually – tracking things on need to review, now at 5 year.
Developed 'glossary' which helped interdisciplinary communication. Guidance didn't show clear enough paths to requesting funding. It may take 20 years to know if reaching targets.

*Specifics: What specific guidance changes might have resulted in a better product for this park?*

- Coordinate inter-divisional needs for staff, park wide coordination.
- Budget guidance – identifying projects that can be accomplished under a core ops scenario.

- Comprehensive strategies could be developed for a 1-year period and then reviewed for completeness.
- Consider a 5-year accuracy review to be sure strategies are still on target

*Other comments or observations:*

- No Fundamental Resources and Values (FRVs) established before RSS, would have been helpful.
- Vital signs monitoring in HEHO is not frequent enough for adaptive management.

### Denali National Park and Preserve

*Chapters/ Main Elements: What are the most and least useful elements of the RSS?*

- Recognized strengths: Grouping of strategies, table linking projects to FRVs, ranking system for prioritizing projects, budget tables by major fund source, status of knowledge, program integration, and summary document. Budget tables helpful for planning and framework for park funding.
- Weaker: target condition definition.
- Integrate with FRVs was very clear and provided focus for strategies.
- Summary document was highlighted as a significant strength.
- Budget tables useful, could compare with capacity and defined outstanding need.
- Most useful outcomes: collaboration among divisions, linked projects to FRV's, prioritization, showed relation to all park projects.

*Innovations: Are there of innovative ideas from the RSS worth adopting programmatically?*

- Grouping strategies and 'overview box" – unifying themes.
- Linkage tables to FRVs.
- Ranking system with numbers, banding of projects by priority.
- Communication document, summary for public and stakeholders.
- Budget tables presentation.
- Linkage tables of project to FRVs.

*Guidance: What are the reported and observed strengths and weakness of guidance?*

- Target vs. standard vs. reference conditions – park took cautious approach when existing target didn't exist (GMP, Alaska National Interest Land Claims Act (ANILCA), etc.).
- Park programs are all well integrated.
- Disparity between how guidance can be implemented in various park types.
- Public involvement guidance not adequate.
- Stretching planning thought out to 20 years was a valuable exercise.
- Budget tables provided good framework to plan by funding source.
- Recommended identifying expert reviewers who are good science strategists.

*Specifics: What specific guidance changes might have resulted in a better product for this park?*

- Defining how narrow the strategies should be – just FRVs or all science needs.
- Clarifying role of management zones, DENA did not use zones.
- Public process guidance not well enough defined.
- Streamline expert review.
- Clarity definitions of target vs. standard vs. reference – park used conditions derived from other NEPA documents and state regulations where possible.

*Other comments or observations:*

- DENA had significant staff and funds to complete their RSS.
- DENA had significant management support, allowing for staff focus and implementation.
- New guidance should differentiate laundry list to meet objectives vs. capacity constraints
- NEPA issues came up over definition of standards more than over prioritization or schedule.
- Need to clarify balance of strategies to be feasible vs. all that are scientifically recommended.

### Guadalupe Mountains National Park

*Chapters/ Main Elements: What are the most and least useful elements of the RSS?*

- Budget exercise had good and bad elements in the park's view, but identified potential sequencing, partnerships, etc. Identification of FRVs, development of comprehensive strategies, and putting them on a calendar were the most useful items for the park.
- Large ID team helped the park identify all resources
- Timing and priority schedule were very useful to the park.
- The budget table was the least useful item to the park – integrating with the timeline tables would have been a helpful improvement.
- Reviewers liked the park resource description, it didn't go overboard, but could have included more references.

*Innovations: Are there of innovative ideas from the RSS worth adopting programmatically?*

- Expanded team for indicators workshops, broad civic engagement.
- Workshop manual.
- Status of knowledge was a good example.
- Foundation incorporated in RSS.
- Park liked a loose leaf format to accommodate regular updates.
- Denver Service Center was critical for project management and production.
- 1st part of RSS is foundation document (i.e. combine).
- Included county planners on team, good example of wide input.

*Guidance: What are the reported and observed strengths and weakness of guidance?*

- GUMO found definitions in guidance useful, consistently applied terminology.
- Emphasis of civic engagement useful.
- Role of SME's useful.
- Hard to identify target values for many indicators.
- GUMO found it effective to let the planners do format and facilitation and park staff to do content.
- Park underestimated the time needed to complete RSS.
- GUMO didn't specifically address climate change.

*Specifics: What specific guidance changes might have resulted in a better product for this park?*

- More sharing of ideas and approaches among RSS parks would have been extremely helpful.
- Could have organized strategies and grouped by priority.

*Other comments or observations:*

- Interpretive themes not really in RSS, might improve in that area.
- Electronic versions preferred, only printed a few.
- Wilderness >50% of park so was inherently addressed.
- Expert reviews need strategic planning viewpoint and a thorough understanding of partnerships

### Monocacy National Battlefield

*Chapters/ Main Elements: What are the most and least useful elements of the RSS?*

- Strategic planning for out years not done in other resource documents.
- Indicators, reference condition, management target were highlights for park.
- MONO presents desired conditions early in document.
- Followed template fairly closely and it worked well for them, timeline was challenging to format and manipulate.
- RSS was a collection of institutional knowledge not before compiled.
- Strategic plan for resources – "one stop shopping".

*Innovations: Are there of innovative ideas from the RSS worth adopting programmatically?*

- Extensive narrative in strategies sections was well received.
- Nicely formatted charts.
- Appendices detailing how they derived indicators and targets in matrix.
- Clear identification of dependencies.
- Facilitator was very important for keeping process going.
- Didn't find zone approach helpful.
- Equal natural and cultural involvement critical.

- Highly readable, narrative strategies, numbering system innovative.

*Guidance: What are the reported and observed strengths and weakness of guidance?*

- Management zone approach not useful to park.
- Formatting described in guidance worked well but tables challenging.
- Any new guidance should use language which is more relevant to cultural resources.
- Didn't take guidance too literally.

*Specifics: What specific guidance changes might have resulted in a better product for this park?*

- If park knew the flexibility around guidance, they might have deviated to help make it work for park with available and level of information.
- Having a strategic document for funding needs is significant benefit to cultural resource management.
- The RSS integrates among existing and somewhat disparate cultural programs.
- Park thought a 10-year document may have better suited their needs.

*Other comments or observations:*

- A revision every 3-5 years seems appropriate to the park.
- Liked that it was a value-based approach and not a threat-based approach to planning.
- They recommend simplifications, or simpler options for smaller parks.

**Point Reyes National Seashore**

*Chapters/ Main Elements: What are the most and least useful elements of the RSS?*

- The park found it extremely useful to develop a high level of detail provided in the comprehensive list of activities proposed as part of the strategies.
- The park found little value in the budget exercise. It would have been more valuable if the RSS produced a timeline showing what the park intends to do over the next 10 years, what the existing staff will be working on, what a staffing chart would look like if fully built out the park needs.
- Status of knowledge a good snapshot of current knowledge.

*Innovations: Are there of innovative ideas from the RSS worth adopting programmatically?*

- Used 'objectives' rather than desired conditions to not be in conflict with draft GMP.
- Managed by database, allowing for searching and sorting as desired.
- Regrouped by activity type at end of document.
- Climate change section and hedging strategies were a unique approach which specifically identified which activities had value regardless of climate change impacts.
- Adopting a loose leaf format to facilitate easy updates and the idea that the RSS is a living document.

- Summary table showing status of knowledge by FRVs.
- Used different terms than guidance including attributes (not objectives).
- Documented progress toward accomplishing targets.
- Hedging=proactive approach to climate change
- 200 activities to promote 63 objectives, more than other RSSs.

*Guidance: What are the reported and observed strengths and weakness of guidance?*

- As a model test park, PORE tried some alternative approaches that intentionally deviated from the guidance.
- Didn't use any calendar or scheduling tool.
- Didn't show costs or full-time employees (FTEs) needed to implement.
- Recommended adding effectiveness monitoring (change of resource to activity).
- Triage needed, priorities are a key part of document.
- RSS would be stronger if it shows what is available and what is needed to accomplish the strategies.
- Additional guidance needed on scope of the status of knowledge section.

*Specifics: What specific guidance changes might have resulted in a better product for this park?*

- The guidance on desired conditions and targets leads parks to promise more in monitoring all of the park resources than is reasonable. PORE recommends doing effectiveness monitoring to determine whether efforts are having a positive effect. Substantially different than embarking on long-term monitoring of all of our FRVs to see if they meeting targets.
- More detail on cultural resource status and targets needed, could have developed better inter-relationships more robust targets.

*Other comments or observations:*

- Close to guidance, just modified nomenclature and layout.
- RSS as vehicle to unify park programs around core goals.
- Specifically identified climate change and hedging activities.

### Chattahoochee River National Recreation Area

*Chapters/ Main Elements: What are the most and least useful elements of the RSS?*

- Status of knowledge very extensive, but maybe some should have been in an appendix to increase readability.

*Innovations: Are there of innovative ideas from the RSS worth adopting programmatically?*

- Coordinated resource indicators table with I&M program and Natural Resource Condition Assessment.

- Keeping to guidance, not too much many innovations.

*Guidance: What are the reported and observed strengths and weakness of guidance?*

- Template allowed them to use 'plug and play' approach. Very important for parks with smaller staffs to be able to collect and insert data without redefining strategic planning process.

Specifics: What specific guidance changes might have resulted in a better product for this park?

- Context: think of park management successors and what information we can we give them to start.

Should focus guidance on gathering data for fundamental resources and not all resources, at least for parks with smaller staffs.

# References

Denn, Marie, 2009. *Lessons Learned from Pilot RSS Parks.* 16 pages. Unpublished, but available at http://www1.nrintra.nps.gov/planning/.

Malone, Patrick, and Cahill, Kerri, 2008. *Lessons Learned from the Pilot Resource Stewardship Strategy (RSS) Projects for Improving the Park Planning Program.* A report submitted from the Denver Service Center (DSC) Planning Division to the WASO Office of Park Planning & Special Studies (PPSS) and other relevant program offices. 10 pages, available at http://www1.nrintra.nps.gov/planning/.

Mason, Gary, 2007. Resource Stewardship Strategy: *A New Program Plan.* Unpublished briefing sheet, available at http://www1.nrintra.nps.gov/planning/.

# Appendix 1 – Status of Resource Stewardship Strategies

## Resource Stewardship Strategy Status
Last updated September 30, 2010

| Unit | Code | Region | Contact | Start FY | Finish FY | Method | Status |
|------|------|--------|---------|----------|-----------|--------|--------|
| Herbert Hoover NHS | HEHO | MWR | Sheri Middlemis-Brown | 2006 | 2007 | Self | Complete |
| Denali NP & P | DENA | AKR | Philip Hooge, Asst Supt | 2006 | 2009 | Self | Complete |
| Guadalupe Mountains NP | GUMO | IMR | Fred Armstrong, Res Mgr | 2007 | 2009 | DSC - Malone | Complete |
| Effigy Mounds NM | EFMO | MWR | Rodney Rovang | | * | Self | Process terminated |
| Monocacy NB | MONO | NCR | Andrew Banasik, Joy Beasley | 2006 | 2010* | Self | Near final draft |
| Chattahoochee River NRA | CHAT | SER | Rick Slade, Chief of CR and NR Joel Brumm, NR ProMgr | 2007 | 2011* | DSC – Larissa Read | Draft complete, ready for ex review |
| New River Gorge NR | NERI | NER | Debbie Darden, Dept Supt; Scott Stonum, Res Mgr | | 2011 | Penn State - Carolyn Mahan | In Process |
| Point Reyes NS | PORE | PWR | Marie Denn, Ecologist | 2006 | 2010 | Self | ExReview Draft |
| Klondike Gold Rush NHP | KLGO | AKR | Dave Schirokauer | 2009 | 2011* | DSC-Malone | Park Review Draft |
| Sand Creek Massacre NHS | SAND | IMR | Alden Miller, Supt | 2009 | 2011* | DSC - Thomas | PA complete |
| Lava Beds NM | LABE | PWR | Dave Larsen, Chief of Res Heather Rickleff, Res Spc | 2010 | 2011* | Self-hired Heather | Started formally 3/1/10 |
| Abraham Lincoln Birthplace NHS | ABLI | SER | Keith Pruitt, Supt | 2010 | 2010* | DSC – Craig Cellar | Kickoff Mar10 |
| Valley Forge NHP | VAFO | NER | Kristina Heister, Res Mgr Deirdre Gibson, Planning/cr | 2008 | 2012 | NRPC-Dave Vana-Miller | In process |
| Pecos NHP | PECO | IMR | Nancy Skinner, Acting Supt Daniel Jacobs, Chief Ranger | 2010 | 2011 | CESU – CSU Fiege/Bzdek | Strategies Wkshp Nov 2010 |

| | | | | | | | |
|---|---|---|---|---|---|---|---|
| Bering Land Bridge NP | BELA | AKR | | 2010 | | | Insufficient funds for FY10 start |
| Pea Ridge NMP | PERI | MWR | | 2010 | | | Insufficient funds for FY10 start |
| Catoctin Mountain Park | CATO | NCR | Mel Poole, Supt Sean Denniston, Res Mgr | 2010 | | | Insufficient funds for FY10 start |
| Channel Islands NP | CHIS | PWR | Kate Faulkner | | | | Insufficient funds for FY10 start |
| Fort Donelson NB | FODO | SER | Steve McCoy, Supt Bill Barley, Res Mgr | 2010 | | Possible CESU with UGA | Self-funded, starting in FY10 |
| Fort Union | FOUN | MWR | Kevin Eads, Res Mgr | | | | |
| Minuteman NM | MIMA | NER | | | | | |
| Boston Harbor Islands NRA | BOHA | NER | Mark Albert | | | | In process |
| Curecanti NRA | CURE | IMR | Ken Stahlnecker, Res Mgr | | | CESU | Park said they could start in FY10, no confirmation from NRSS |

*Project performance timeline adversely affected by funding issues (e.g. delays in authorization, carry-over funds, withdrawal-conversion of 30% funds to REA 20% funds).
I = Park independently pursuing RSS

# Appendix 2 – Workshop Participants

## PARTICIPANTS
## NPS Resource Stewardship Strategy Workshop
April 13-15, 2010
Fort Collins Hilton - Ft Collins, Colorado

**Parks**

| | | |
|---|---|---|
| Guy Adema | Denali NP&P | Physical Scientist |
| Fred Armstrong | Guadalupe Mountains NP | Resource Management Specialist |
| Andrew Banasik | Monocacy NB | Natural Resource Program Manager |
| Joy Beasley | Monocacy NB | Cultural Resource Program Manager |
| Kathy Billings | Pecos NHP | Superintendent |
| Marie Denn | Point Reyes NS | Aquatic Ecologist |
| Cat Hoffman | Olympic NP | Chief, Natural Resources; |
| Philip Hooge | Denali NP&P | Assistant Superintendent |
| *Carolyn Mahan | Penn State (NERI contractor) | Prof. of Biology and Environ. Science |
| Steven McCoy | Fort Donelson NB | Superintendent |
| *Sherry Middlemis-Brown | Herbert Hoover NHS | Biologist |
| Heather Rickleff | Lava Beds NM | Resource Specialist |
| Dave Schirokauer | Klondike Gold Rush NHP | Natural Resource Program Manager |
| Rick Slade | Chattahoochee NRA | Chief, Science and Resource Management |

**Natural Resource Stewardship and Science Directorate (NRSS)**

| | | |
|---|---|---|
| Steve Fancy | Inventory & Monitoring | I&M Program Leader |
| Jeff Albright | Water Resources | NR Condition Assessment Prgrm Manager |
| Gary Mason | NRSS | Natural Resource Specialist |
| Dave Vana-Miller | Water Resources | Branch Chief, WR Planning and Evaluation |
| Jerry Mitchell | Biological Resources | Division Chief, BRMD |
| Bill Jackson | Water Resources | Division Chief, WRD |
| Don Weeks | Water Resources | Hydrologist |
| Andrea Stacy | Air Resources | Environmental Protection Specialist |

**Regions**

| | | |
|---|---|---|
| Jill Cowley | Intermountain Region | Historical Landscape Architect |
| Jay Goldsmith | Pacific West Region | Asst Regional Chief Scientist |
| Dave Reynolds | Northeast Region | Chief, NR and Science |
| Cheryl Sams-O'neill | Northeast Region | Landscape Architect, Resource Planner |
| Jeanne Schaaf | WASO CR representative | Chief, LACL Cultural Resources |
| John Sowl | Midwest Region | Landscape Ecologist |
| Pam Benjamin | Intermountain Region | Vegetation Ecologist |

**Denver Service Center**

| | | |
|---|---|---|
| Patrick Malone | Denver Service Center | Planner, Natural Resource Specialist |
| Larissa Read | Denver Service Center | Planner, Natural Resource Specialist |

*via teleconference

# Appendix 3 – Workshop Agenda

## AGENDA
## NPS Resource Stewardship Strategy Workshop

April 13-15, 2010
Fort Collins Hilton - Ft Collins, Colorado

| **Tuesday, April 13 – Focus: Pilot Review** |
| --- |

INTRODUCTION

    8:00    Coffee
    8:30    Introductions, Logistics, Agenda Review

    9:00    Workshop Goals and Overview of RSS Review (Adema)

**GOAL: Provide recommendations for implementation of a Resource Stewardship Strategy program based on the experience of pilot efforts.**

1. Assess which elements of the pilot RSS's are most valuable to parks.
2. Define purpose of RSS's and their role in the NPS planning framework.
3. Refine RSS guidance to efficiently produce quality plans.
4. Develop ideas for improved NPS Resource Stewardship policy.
5. Identify the core functions of a NPS Resource Planning program.

    Status of RSS pilots (Adema)
    Evolution of RSS and original RSS objectives (Gary Mason)

    10:00    Break

PILOT REVIEW

Pilot's will present:
1. Your park's process - why you did an RSS, process for completion (staff, time, sme's, cost, etc), review, etc
2. Overview of your park's RSS - structure, unique elements, most challenging part, etc
3. Most useful elements of your RSS to park management
4. Lease useful elements of your RSS and/or least efficient to complete
5. HIGHLIGHT - an element of your RSS which you find particularly innovative, practical, or interesting
6. Specific areas in which you found the guidance and resulting RSS elements very useful and instructive
7. Specific areas in which the guidance was not helpful to your process or did not provide adequate instruction
8. What would you have improved or added if you had more time
9. What's next - how has your park used the RSS to date, further plans for implementation, plans to keep RSS current
10. Reflections - was it worth it?

**Participants will record thematic observations for each pilot in 4 areas:**

5) Pilot RSS Elements: What are the most and least useful elements of each pilot product?

6) Innovations: Are there of innovative ideas from a pilot worth adopting programmatically?
7) Guidance: What are the reported and observed strengths and weakness of guidance?
8) Specifics: What specific change in guidance would have produced a better product?

---

**Tuesday, April 13 – continued**

---

| | |
|---|---|
| 10:20 | Herbert Hoover (Sherry Middlemis-Brown) |
| 11:00 | Denali (Philip Hooge) |
| 11:45 | Lunch |
| 13:00 | Guadalupe Mountains (Fred Armstrong) |
| 13:30 | Point Reyes (Marie Denn) |
| 14:00 | Break |
| 14:20 | Monocacy (Andrew Banasik) |
| 14:40 | Chattahoochee (Rick Slade) |
| 15:00 | **What are the consensus and unique observations from pilot reports?** |
| 16:00 | Adjourn |
| 16:10 | Optional – depart for 4:30 tour of New Belgium Brewing Company |

---

**Wednesday, April 14 – Focus: Interdisciplinary Integration and Planning Framework**

| | |
|---|---|
| 8:00 | Coffee |
| 8:15 | Summary of consensus ideas from Tuesday pilot review (5 minutes per group) |
| 8:45 | Lessons Learned Summaries (Malone and Denn) - Common themes, strongest points |
| 9:15 | Guidance Review: Overview original RSS guidance of development (Middlemis-Brown) |

9:30
**(breakout).**

**Develop specific recommendations for improving upon pilot RSS's**

1. What are the minimum elements of a successful RSS?
2. Which pilot provides an ideal example of each RSS chapter/section?
3. What are good examples of value-added RSS elements and why?
4. What are the strengths and deficiencies of the handbook and template?
5. What are ideas for RSS standard products – scope, size, format, and audience?
    (technical, educational, standard executive summary and or tables)

| 10:00-10:15 | Break |
| --- | --- |
| 10:30 | Presentation and discussion of recommendations from each breakout group |

**11:10**  **How do park's achieve interdisciplinary integration in resource planning?**
   Pecos approach to a fully integrated RSS (Kathy Billings)
   Klondike Goldrush approach to integration (Dave Schirokauer)
   Integration of Cultural Resource Data to the RSS's (Cheryl Sams-O'neill)

   Discussion: Can RSS process or structure be improved to meet needs of all resource
activities?

**12:00**  Lunch

**13:00**  **What is the ideal relationship of RSS's to other planning and evaluation
steps?**

   RSS within larger planning framework (Gary Mason)
   RSS Relation to NRCA and Park's Canada approach (Jeff Albright)
   Recent developments in Condition Reporting and report cards (Steve Fancy)

   Discussion:    Order: Is there a model resource planning timeline?
            Preparation: Are there recommended pre-requisites for completing an
      RSS?
            Roll-up: How to communicate RSS targets and strategies to mixed
      audience?
            Implementation: What are the follow-on steps and tie to funding?
            Relevance: How parks keep RSS's current without becoming
overwhelmed?

**14:30-14:50**  Break

**15:10**  **How do other planning efforts best integrate and complement the RSS?**
   ▪ Point Reyes RSS approach to climate change (Marie Denn)
   ▪ Climate change scenario planning, adaptation, vulnerability assessments.
     Overview & case study  (Cat Hoffman)
   ▪ At what stage are other planning products most valuable?

**16:00**  **What is the goal of Expert Review?**
   Who should review? Best practices and minimums. Overall document vs specific
sections?

**16:30**  Adjourn

---

**Thursday, April 15 – Focus: Guidance Details, RSS Completion, and Program Operations**

| 8:00 | Coffee |
| --- | --- |
| 8:15 | Integration: example of scientific support for holistic approach (Schaaf) |

**8:25**  **What is the best way to complete an RSS for various park situations?**
   Denver Service Center approach to RSS completion (Malone and Schirokauer)
   Park-led but cooperative approach to completion (Billings)
   Cooperator/Contractor approach and experience – New River (Mahan)
            Discussion:    What are the factors for success for each process?

|  |  | Could a preliminary feasibility scoping provide direction to parks w/o |
| an RSS? | | |

| 9:10 | **What is the role of WASO Specialists to assist park RSS's?** |
| | NRPC support and facilitation of RSS process, current situation (Weeks, Vana-Miller() |
| | NRPC participation – providing focused technical guidance (Andrea Stacey) |

|  | Discussion: | Timing: What is the right time to incorporate SME's and WASO |
| specialists? | | |

|  | | Need: What technical guidance would be most helpful to parks? |
|  | | Product: Is it reasonable to have a core set of technical suggestions? |

| 9:40 | Expert Review:  What structure will make expert review timely and worthwhile? |
| | Requirements or recommendations? |
| | Who is final signatory of RSS? |

| 10:00 | Break |
| 10:20 | Prioritization |

| 10:40 | Social Indicators |

| 11:00 | **RSS Program management: What support and leadership is ideal?** |
| | Discussion: | What should be the organizational home and role of program manager? |
| | | What are regional needs for successful program implementation? |
| | | What is the minimum support parks need to complete an RSS? |

| 11:30 | Implementation: should there be a tie to funding? |
| | Recommended revisit rate and/or periodic report? |
| | Importance of comprehensive strategies. |
| | Should strategies by loose commitments, hopeful goals, or idealized visions? |
| | Consensus on guidance for management zones |
| | Activity vs Project definition |

| 12:15 | Lunch and early departures |

| 13:00 | Director's Order: Any significant additions or subtractions recommended? Key elements? |

| 13:15 | Communication Plan – provide feedback on how to communicate our recommendations |
| | Next steps – review meeting product, ideas for maintaining momentum and interest |

| **13:40** | **Define summary message and recommendations for NLC, NRAG, CRAG.** |

| 14:10 | Assess unfinished discussion topics – workgroups: exec summary, gant/budget tool |
| | Suggestions for short-term follow-up |
| | Summary Comments |
| 14:30 | Adjourn |

# Appendix 4 – Regional Contacts

Regional RSS contacts as of spring 2011.

| | |
|---|---|
| Alaska Region | Joan Darnell |
| Pacific West Region | Jay Goldsmith |
| Midwest Region | John Sowl |
| National Capital Region | Diane Pavek |
| Northeast Region | David Reynolds<br>Shaun Eyring |
| Southeast Region | R. Dale McPherson |
| Intermountain Region | Bonnie Semro<br>Jill Cowley |

NPS 999/108032, June 2011